I0260489

A HEAD ABOVE THE REST

The Long and Short of It

By Dr. Diane P. Fleming

A Head Above the Rest

Copyright © 2025 by
Dr. Diane P. Fleming
All rights reserved

No part of this publication may be reproduced, stored in a retrieval system or transmitted in any way by any means, electronic, mechanical, photocopy, recording or otherwise without the prior permission of the author except as provided by USA copyright law.

This is a work of non-fiction.
Book design copyright © 2025 by
Dr. Diane P. Fleming

All rights reserved
Published in the United States of America
ISBN 979-8-9924138-0-9 (Paperback)
2.27.25

Learn more about Diane and her love for books and stories at
www.dpfwriter.com

THANK YOU!

I want to thank Judith Dubin for her keen eye and many suggestions. I appreciate your guidance and wisdom.

Dr. Deb Daiek has encouraged and guided both of my books, which I appreciate.

Lor Bingham, my editor and owner of Calicio Editing Services in England, has been a gift. She answers my questions and puts my books in excellent order.

I sincerely thank Vivian Jenkins for her constant encouragement, support, and friendship in this endeavor. Thank you for always being there.

Dedication

This book is dedicated to my Mother and Grandmother who have always supported and encouraged me throughout my life.

A special hug to the love of my life for your continued support and encouragement. Your skill and ability are unique gifts that are always shared unselfishly.

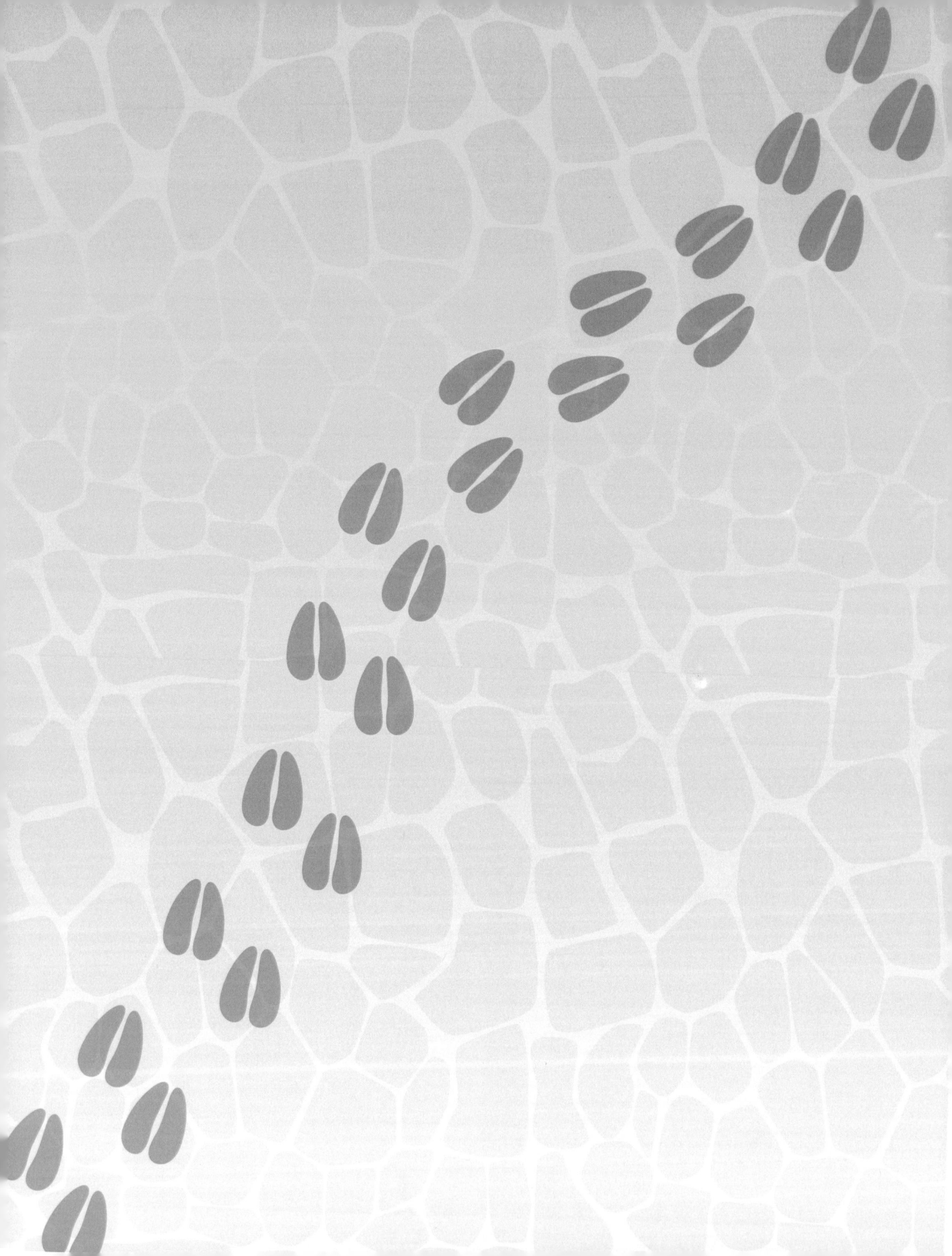

Do You Know?

Giraffes are the tallest animal on Earth.

Most giraffes live in Africa.

How tall are giraffes?

Female giraffes grow up to 14 feet tall. | Male giraffes grow up to 18 feet tall.

Young giraffes are called calves. They weigh 150-200 pounds at birth.

This is a newborn giraffe.

Aren't these babies cute?
They can stand up
15 minutes after birth.

Giraffe Families

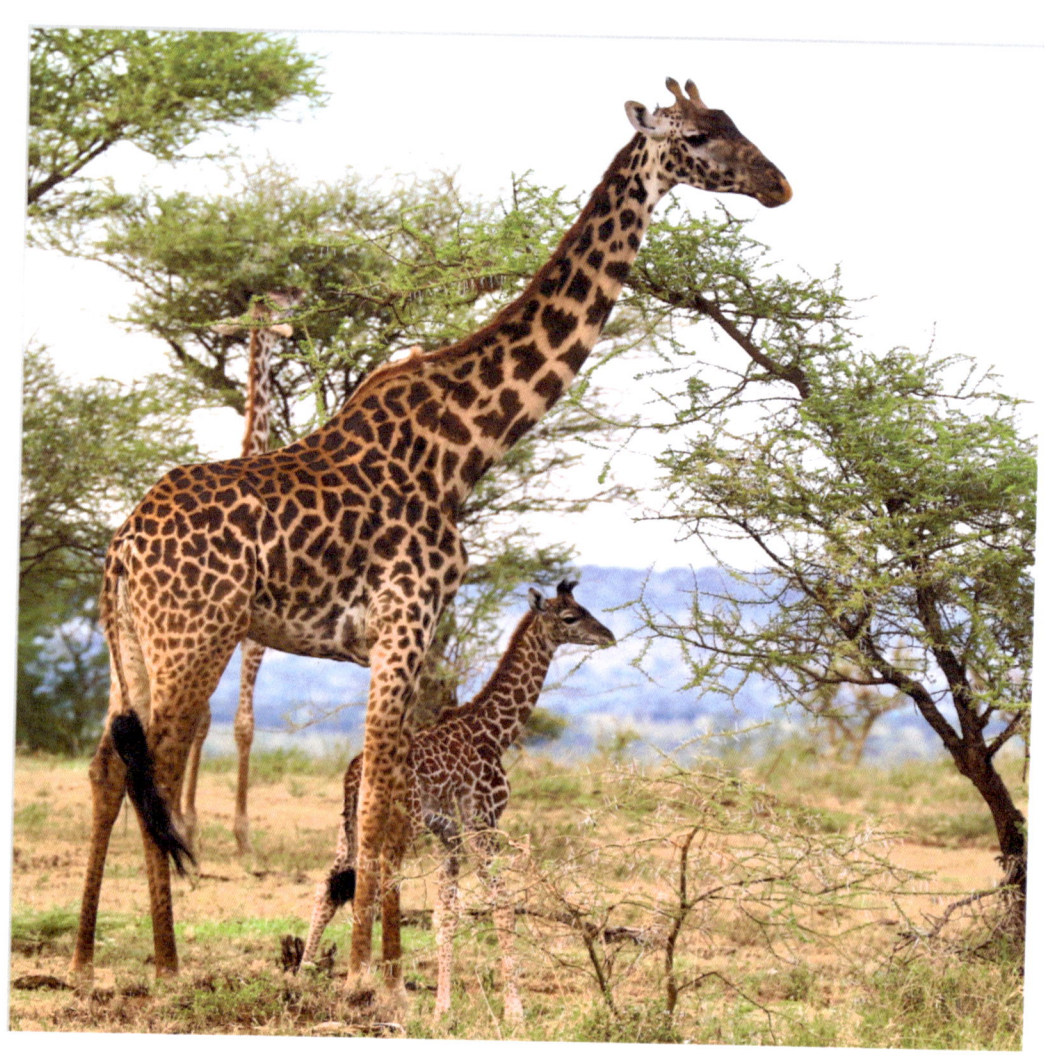

Mom and baby.

Dad, Mom, and baby.

Do You Know?

How long is a giraffe's tail?

16

Look at this giraffe's tail.

Their tails can grow as long as eight feet.

Giraffes eat leaves and fruit from tall Acacia trees.

What do you eat?

Yum!

Do You Know?

How do giraffes drink water?

They bend their front knees.

Giraffes drinking water.

How do you drink water?

Do You Know? How do giraffes sleep?

Most giraffes sleep standing up.

Giraffes only need 5 to 30 minutes of sleep in a day.

Sometimes, they sit down when they sleep.

Giraffes have tall legs; some are six feet long.

Do You Know?

How long are giraffe tongues?

Giraffe tongues can be purple, blue, or black. They can be 18-22 inches long. That's about as long as your arm!

Giraffes have extra-long necks.

Giraffes and humans have the same number of vertebrae in their neck.

They both have seven vertebrae.

All giraffes have two bony bumps on the top of their head.

They are called ossicones and they are covered with skin and fuzzy hair.

Older male giraffes often get an additional bony deposit called a basil knob.

Giraffes have a sloping back. Their front legs are longer than their back legs.

Giraffes eyes are the size of golf balls.

Does this giraffe look happy?

This giraffe is happy.

How do you look when you are happy?

Giraffe spots are like fingerprints; no two are alike.

These two giraffes have different patterns and colors.

All giraffes have manes from the base of the neck to the shoulders.

Giraffes can weigh more than 3,500 pounds.

That's about the same weight as a small truck!

You can only see giraffes at a zoo unless your parents take you to Africa.

GLOSSARY

Acacia Tree - a type of tree, often found in warm places like Africa and Australia, with small, feathery leaves and fluffy, yellow or white flower clusters, sometimes with thorns.

Basil Knob - A bony deposit on some older male giraffes.

Calves - What a baby giraffe is called.

Mane - Heavy hair coming from neck area.

Ossicones - Hard bone covered with skin and fur.

Patterns - A camouflage design on a giraffe that keeps animals safe from prey.

Tongues - Used to pull leaves off trees, also for cleaning their eyes and ears.

Vertebrae - Bones of spine or backbone.

RESOURCES

The Giraffe Conservation Foundation (GCF) — https://giraffeconservation.org/facts-about-giraffe/how-long-is-a-giraffes-tongue-what-color-is-it

Sykes, D. (January 18, 2015) Giraffes: 51 facts that will fascinate your kids — https://archive.org/details/giraffes51fascin0000debo

National Geographic Kids: https://www.natgeokids.com/uk/discover/animals/general-animals/ten-giraffe-facts

Giraffe Facts for Kids: https://factsforkids.com/giraffe

Baby giraffe Learns How to Run | The Secret Life of the Zoo | Nature Bites: https://youtu.be/ZegmTjAbO9E?si=HN_OBNpgRR23k6gn

Leafy Lunchtime with giraffes | Sam's Zookeeper Challenge: https://www.youtube.com/watch?v=Jwk2Z4E3Xpw

THANK YOU!

Your purchase supports this cause.

10% of the book's sales will be donated to support giraffes. Donations will be sent to the **Giraffe Conservation Foundation**

Kwa heri* from Africa!
(*Swahili for "Good Bye")

ACKNOWLEDGMENTS

Thank you to my friends for allowing the use of giraffe pictures for

A Head Above the Rest

Leslie Brown
Cynthia Cockrel
Deb Daiek
Denise Daniel
Alex J. Diaz-Rivera
Bev Dietch
Judith Dubin
Lynn Hermann Rodd
Shari Kalt
Bruce Mazzola
Ed Morykwas
Paul Piper
Sherry Rochelle
Maurice Sanders
Carol Shelton
Pam Wilkins

―――――――――

A special thanks to the Design Team of Tammy Monroe and Mame Hill.

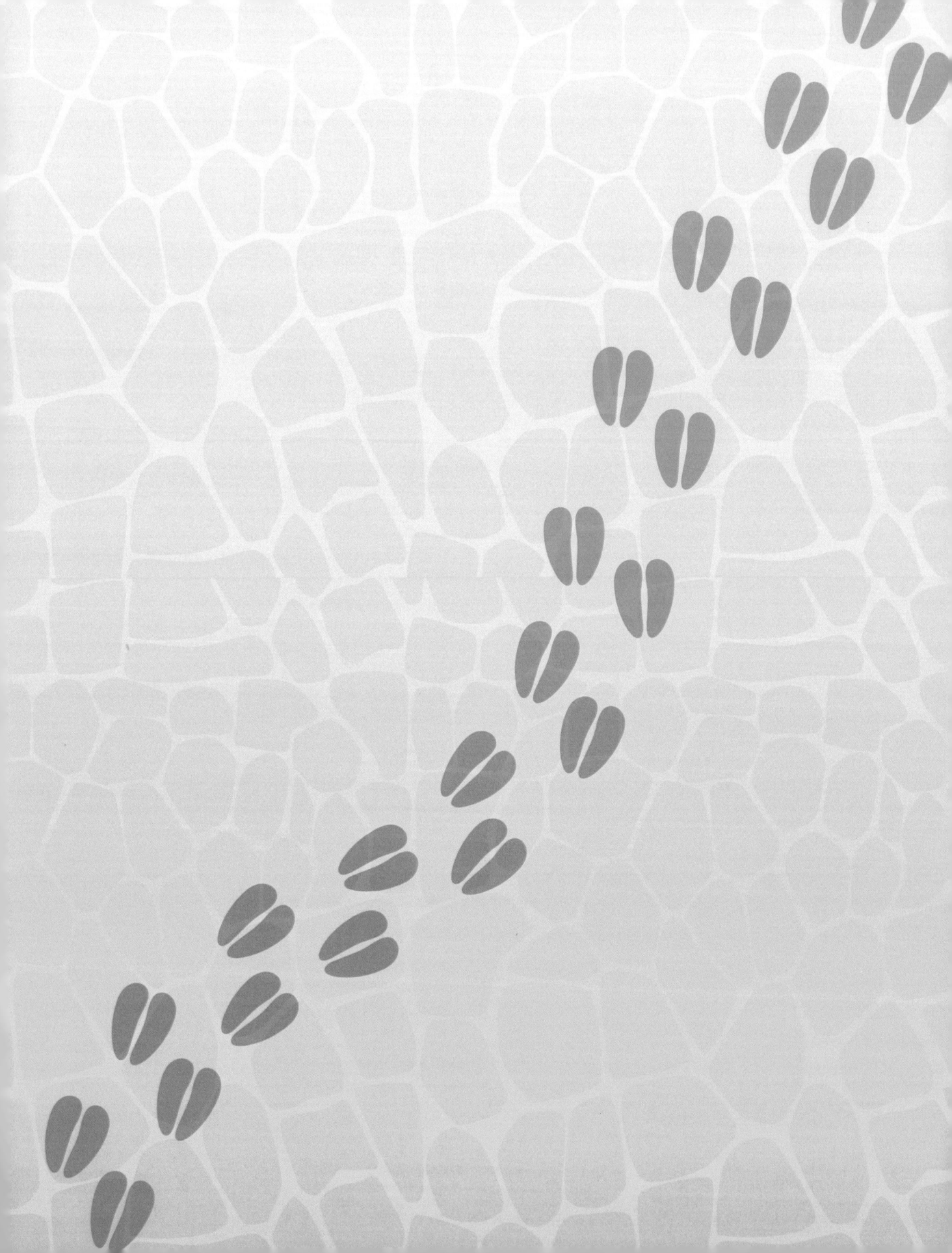

www.ingramcontent.com/pod-product-compliance
Lightning Source LLC
Chambersburg PA
CBRC101144030426
42337CB00008B/66